No Man's Land

No Man's Land

Poems

Logan C. Jones

RESOURCE *Publications* · Eugene, Oregon

NO MAN'S LAND
Poems

Resource Publications
An Imprint of Wipf and Stock Publishers
199 W. 8th Ave., Suite 3
Eugene, OR 97401

www.wipfandstock.com

ISBN 13: 978-1-62564-747-4

Manufactured in the U.S.A.

05/07/2014

To Kelli

We would rather be ruined than changed

—W. H. AUDEN

You must change your life

—RAINER MARIA RILKE

Contents

Acknowledgments

I THANK THE EDITORS of the following publications in which the poems below previously appeared.

Healing Ministry: "To Speak of Fire"; "End-Stage"

Hobart Park: "Bach Will Be Enough"

The Journal of Pastoral Care & Counseling: "The Antidote to Pain"; "James and Bessie Tate"; "God Bless You, Mary Oliver"

Main Street Rag: "No Man's Land"

The Progressive Christian: "Revolution"; "Under a Full Moon on Christmas Eve"; "The Other Advent"; "Elvis Has Left the Building" (originally titled "Elvis is Dead . . . Really")

No Man's Land

The old farm house seemed huge,
mansion-like in all its secrets and
out-buildings with their weathered boards.
His room was upstairs
where it was hot and musty,
bathed in a yellow haze of light.
An old trunk kept his gas mask,
cartridge belt, and helmet.

The helmet carried a dent
from a sniper's bullet
or so the story went in the family.

These war relics made for great battles
in the backyard where we would climb out
of the trenches, going over the top
into No Man's Land. Artillery shells would
burst overhead as tanks led the assault.
There would always be a mustard gas attack
which would leave us stricken and
flailing on the ground where we would
end up laughing. These battles
were epic and we never ran out
of tobacco sticks for rifles.
Our casualties always got up for lunch.

My grandfather was a sergeant
in a machine gun company
with the American Expeditionary Force
in France.

I never heard him speak of his war
and I never speak
of mine.

The Antidote to Pain

for Shannon Davenport

The antidote to pain is not anesthesia.
The antidote to pain is poetry.

And poetry takes time and space
and silence and dreams.

But before there can be poetry
there has to be stories:

stories of hunger
of craziness
of shame
of a father long dead
of healing the sick
of casting out demons
of taking a stand
of finding a long forgotten path.

But before there can be stories
there has to be mercy,

sweet

      life-giving

mercy.

Questions at Mid-Life

What am I hungry for?
What is missing?
What am I seeking?
What do I need?
Where can I find it?
Do I want to be healed?

More:

Why am I ashamed and embarrassed by my own neediness?
Why do I try to hide it?
When will I stop living like I have something to prove?
Why does mercy have to be so hard on me?
Why do I feel so unworthy at times?
Why do I settle for crumbs?

Rilke said, Live the questions.
Well, screw him.

Preparing for the Moon Rise

In the late afternoon
time of the fading sun,
I watch six hawks
glide on high currents.
With quick movement of their wings,
they soar up and down, right and left
with intent and delight.

Later in the evening,
I realize what they were doing:
They were pulling the moon
from its sleep and into the sky
to bless the world,
and even me.

I never knew the moon
needed help.

Maybe we all do.

Revolution

Nobody likes it
when the summons comes from God.

Certainly not Judas.
Everything changes with God.
Turned
up-side down,
and inside out,
this becomes that; that is now this.

The first become last.
Children enter the kingdom.
Demons are cast out.
The sick are healed.
Surely it is the acceptable year
of the Lord.

I wonder if Judas knew
what he was called to do.
If he did,
surely it was a terrible knowledge.
Maybe he was the only one among us
who had the strength
of a broken heart.

We all deny,
doubt,
resist,
flee,
jockey for the favored position.
We all refuse to understand.
We all destroy and hurt.
We all betray.
There is nothing new here.

I wonder if Judas
knew what it would cost
to complete what was
set in motion long ago.

But Judas answered
the summons anyway
and it killed him.

Maybe it is Judas
who sits now
at the right hand
of God,
laughing.

This night,
I count him as friend.

God Bless You, Mary Oliver

after hearing "Thirst"

Maybe it was the words,
or your cadence, or the tone
and timbre of your voice,
or perhaps the gentle space you created.
Maybe it was your impish wisdom.

You took me to a sacred space,
across a threshold
to a place where I had not
visited for a long, long time.

You made it all so simple:
dog, summer day, sun,
        deer, mouse, wren,
                pond, bear, God—

even God.

Gone and Lost the Words

The conversation spins into a dull silence.
I feel out of control.
Then come all the internal messages:

Red alert. Red alert.
Battle stations. Battle stations.

Dive
Dive.
Dive.

Take us down, helmsman.
Get us out of the line of fire.
Prepare for depth charges.

KA-WHOOOMPP. KA-WHOOOMPP.

* * * * * * * *

Where did I learn this?
In the moment, I stutter.
I squirm. I stammer.
My throat catches.
Nothing comes out.
I am empty.

Later, after the battle,
I feel all the sadness,
frustration, and anger.
I feel wounded,
shamed, and utterly defeated.
I wondered if I am ruined beyond repair.

When it matters most,
I am without the words I need.

The words do not come.
They are lost.
The gods mock me
with a cruel irony
as I die a little bit
inside.

* * * * * * *

Is there any hope?
Is there any forgiveness?
Is there another way?

An Inquiry into Courage

Tell me, Spartan, about courage.
You say it is not
the opposite of fear.
It is more;
but what?

Spartan, I have felt my sad, little fear.
I have been embarrassed
and shamed by it.
There. I've said it.

I've heard of your lines of battle,
shields of bronze
radiating in the sun
and striking fear
into marrow and sinew.
I've heard of how your shield protects
your brother who stands
beside you.

But, Spartan, what about these lines?
Who will protect
the line above,
or the lines below,
still unwritten?
Who will carry the shield?
Courage, you say, is being true.

But, Spartan, what of defeat?
Can there be courage in defeat?
You say that is how you grow
as a man,
as a warrior,
as a poet.

Courage, you say, does not yield to defeat.
Courage, you say, protects the lines.

What does courage cost, Spartan?
Surely it is more than blood.
Poetry is easy, they say.
Just open a vein and bleed.
No matter.
The words come only after the feelings,
only after the bronze shield
is held steady and sure.

Tell me, Spartan, will I have enough
courage to be . . . ?

James and Bessie Tate

An old graveyard sits
just down a narrow dirt road
between mile marker 203 and 204
on the Blue Ridge Parkway

There are 12 graves.
A new fence stands guard
around the faded and worn out headstones.
Flowers speak tenderly of the dead.

The headstone for James and Bessie Tate
says they were both born in 1906.
Around the foot of their grave
are six little graves with signs that say

Infants of
Mr. and Mrs. James Tate

No names.
No dates.

James Tate died
when he was 50.
A man can only carry
so much pain in his life.

Maybe burying six infants
was just too much.

Under a Full Moon on Christmas Eve

The neighborhood is quiet this night.
There is no traffic and no sound.
Everyone is waiting and watching.
Everything is silent.

Like so many other Christmas Eves,
there is still no room available
in this broken-down, beat-up, shabby inn of my heart.
All the rooms are taken,

occupied by my old friends
Shame, Fear, Pride, and Weariness.
I wonder if they will ever check out
and make time and space

for Mercy, Forgiveness, Laughter, and Acceptance.
Again this night the cold straw
and the smell of sweat and dung
await Joseph.

The moon watches in the darkness.
In the distance, I hear the Great Star.
Magi are coming.
King Herod stirs.

Come, Thou long expected Jesus.
Jesu, joy of my deepest longings.

The Black Stone, Part III

My mother was a bear
of a woman—
fierce and formidable,
proud and protective.

She shaped me
with a fiery and fearful
love,
doing the best she could
with her own story.

In her fierceness
she gave me
the Black Stone
of her fear.

The messages still haunt:
Don't embarrass the family.
Don't embarrass me.
Don't screw around,
(Keep your pants zipped up).
Don't make mistakes.
We have an image to keep.
On and on she roared.

I was unable to fight back.
I did not know how.
How I wish
I could have stood my ground.
How I wish
I could have roared in return
when I was 17
and battled her
in a life and death struggle.

That would have been
wonderful.

Now, my mother has shrunk.
Age has exacted its toll.
No longer does she roar.

Somewhere deep
in the black stone of fear
is the red fire
of fierceness.

I wonder
if my mother remembers
she was a bear.

Three Voices

Inside of me—
        where exactly, I do not know—
live three voices.

The first voice roars:

        Produce. Do. Achieve.
        You need to attend this meeting.
        Policies and procedures need to be revised.
        There are deadlines to meet and
                reports that need to be completed.
        Budget variances should be corrected.
        Goals for the new fiscal year are due.
        Job descriptions should be re-written.
        Performance evaluations need to take place.
        All is of ultimate importance so
                don't forget anything.
        Your worth as a person depends on this.
        Don't make any mistakes.
        Produce more. Do more. Achieve more.

The middle voice sneers and mocks:

        You fraud.
        You know you will be found out—
                then what?
        You cannot do this work.
        You are a sham, an imposter.
        Shame on you;
                you always make mistakes.
        Who do you think you are?

The lowest voice just whispers:

You are forgiven.
There is mercy.
All shall be well.

The Sea is Forever

The waves, never ceasing,
leave their gift of sand, seaweed,
shell, bone on the shore. The tide
does its work quietly and
without need of praise.
The single pelican stands
watch on the seawall, paying
homage to the Great Source.
The sound of the surf brings
memories of rest. All the
sandcastles will be lost and
the footprints erased.
But the sea, like the tender
mercies of God,

        is forever.

I Will Yield

I want to resist,
and not always comply.
I want to honor my defiance
and not lose my way home.
I want to stand firm,
and not always be the nice guy.
I want to bang up against limits,
and not settle for the easy way out.
I want to hold my ground,
and not cave.
I want to feel my anger and my passion,
and not shrink from my power.
I want to feel the fire of God's terrible mercy,
and not be afraid of who I am.

And when the whirlwind comes,

I will yield.

Maybe Tomorrow

Maybe tomorrow
dreams will be sweeter,
the ache will go away,
and words will come.

Maybe tomorrow
failing will not hurt so much,
rest will be easier,
and I can somehow pray.

Maybe.

The Other Advent

Winter darkness
settles over land
and sky.

Surely this is a time of waiting,
a time of hope,
and a time of anticipation.

There is another
kind of darkness
that also settles:

My mother is lost
in the far darkness
of dementia.

This is a time of confusion.
a time of frustration,
and surely a time of tears.

Somewhere out there
Death is waiting.
Let there be peace—
                    on earth.

December Shadows

This December
go for a walk in the quiet of the night.
There you will find consolation.
Let the cold air quicken your tired bones.
Let the new moon, cradled low in the sky, see you.
Sit by the fire and feel the heart beat of home.

Don't listen to sappy Christmas carols;
they damage your soul.

Don't put up too many decorations;
they invite Herod to reign in his emptiness.

Be careful.
Watch the sky.
Listen for the promise.
Listen for His name
to be whispered
among the shadows.

Lost in Tamarack Pines

Watching and listening to George Winston

Watching him play the piano so easily and gently,
I wonder how he teaches
the archangels?

I feel sweet mercy rise into the air—
simple, with a haunting dissonance
and an exquisite grace.

I am close to genius,
to wisdom,
to gift,
to soul,
to rightness.

I am close to
fire.

Transformation

A middle-aged woman visited me
in a dream.
She interrupted my terribly
unimportant work.

"I want to be baptized," she said.
"I want a new life."

And I said, "Yes."

Easter Moon

On this night long ago, I sat low in the sky,
full and red.
Something was up.
I wanted to see.
It was a night like no other.
It was cold.
The wind blew and
woke up the trees.
But no creatures stirred.
      I think they knew.

Time stood still.
Then the earth shook slightly.
He walked out into the darkness.
He stretched his arms and
rubbed his lower back.
He raised his head to look at me.
      I saw tears in his eyes
      and he smiled.

Then it started:
The angels danced.
The stars bowed.
Michael and Gabriel began to laugh.
They couldn't stop.
They laughed until they cried.
Nothing would ever be the same again,
not after this night.
Now there was Hope.
But then . . .

      people went crazy.

End-Stage

The breathing mask muffles
her sing-song nonsense words.
Arms flail for a moment
then come to a rest by her side.
A hard cough brings distress,
maybe pain.
A wild-eyed grimace crosses her face.
Her eyes close and
sweet rest comes for a moment.

I sit, waiting, not knowing
what to say or what to feel.
It will be over, soon I hope.
I will be sad and relieved
and then sadder still.

I no longer have the need
to fight with her.
That is gone.
She gave me a great gift:
She blessed my leaving home.
She gave me the space to
find my way and become
who I needed to become.
I hope she knows the magnitude
of her giving.

I watch her slip slowly
over the edge.
Let there be forgiveness
between us,
a little mercy,
more love.

Sarasota Bay

Gliding in the sky, the pelican stalls
and suddenly dive bombs into the water.
Bringer of death, he slams into the sea
with a controlled fury. The struggle
underneath, unseen, is but for a moment.

Then he sits floating on the sea
of life, calm and peaceful.
With a burst of happiness
powering his wings, he rises
slowly with gratitude.

Lord, you know that I, too, am trying
to live with such exuberant gratefulness.

To Speak of Fire

To speak of fire is to speak of pain;
to speak of pain is to know

> what it means
> to howl.

To speak of fire is to speak of pain;
to speak of pain is to know

> of the desire
> to surrender.

To speak of fire is to speak of pain;
and to speak of pain is to know

> how to believe

> in waiting.

Elvis Has Left the Building

It's a rather sad sight,
the clamoring for an encore,
all this yelling, "More! More!
Bravo! Bravo!" What's buried inside
all this noise is a shrill unspoken
plea: Stay longer. Please don't go
and leave us. Play all the oldies
we love so we can feel good about
ourselves and what we do. We want
to hang on to what we once had.

Instead of an encore, the opening acts
return, now disguised in different costumes
of new programs designed to entertain.
Mostly they just distract.

The frenzied clapping and stomping,
jumping up and down and waving continue.
But it's not enough.

The princes of the Church just don't get it
that, like Elvis, god has left
the building.

Welcome

I.
In the Blue Ridge Mountains of southwest Virginia, time
 and space are different. The world slows down, and the weight
of work slips off as I drive past the flea markets, antique stores,
the produce stands, and the houses selling gifts and collectibles.

II.
I walk outside in the late afternoon. A three-quarter moon
sits on the ridge, waiting for the sun to sleep.
I see six deer in the yard. Startled to see each other,
we become still, only watching, only breathing.

III.
Two of them, I swear, wagged their white tails at me.
They are in no hurry. They show no fear as a breeze
sweeps across the side of the mountain. Welcome, they say.
Like us, you belong here. In this place, in this time and space,

IV.
home will find you.

Thunder off the Blue Ridge

announces the arrival
of sweet,
life-giving rain.
The grass smiles at this gift.
The clouds sing for joy.
The trees turn
their faces upward,
lifting arms toward
the giving skies.

A deer watches
me from a distance.
She does not flinch.
She says,
I am not afraid of you.
I see into your heart.
You know where hope lies.

I bow to her
and continue on the path.
She turns from me
and walks back into the woods
where her fawn is waiting,
watching, listening,
and learning.

I listen
to the echoes of thunder.
The earth has been renewed
and so have I.
I hear her say again faintly,
Do not be afraid
of the thunder
in your heart.

Drive By

It would have been easy to turn left,
drive down the road a mile or so and
take another left into the grounds
of the continuing care retirement community.

It would have been no problem
to park the car,
enter the Health Care building,
go through the locked door

of the dementia unit and
stop at room 310 on the right.
She would have been sleeping,
curled and knotted up, unrousable;

and if, perchance, she was awake,
she would not know you,
would not be able to form a word,
maybe only smile a bit.

You could have maybe sat with her
for a few moments. The room would
have been hot. All you could have done
is mangle another goddamned goodbye.

Your duty-bound, emotional DNA shouted,
You need to turn left and go see her
but your defiant, rebel-bound soul whispered,
Keep going and do not stop.

There is no way to bridge the chasm.
You are simply left with silence
and the dull ache of
                    distance.

Bach Will Be Enough

The next time I sit in this church
will be for my mother's memorial service.
No longer will she be bent and gnarled,
no longer lost in the dark netherworld
of dementia unable to speak of pain or joy,
unable to feed herself,
unable to host a party,
unable to go shopping,
unable to take a walk,
unable to prepare a feast for family,
unable to work in her garden.

I am not interested in hearing how Jesus
died for our sins or St. Paul's
mumbo-jumbo about eternal life.
It's a meaningless and
bankrupt language now anyway.
I want to hear Bach.

I want to hear Bach
welcome her home.

Bach will be enough.

Pilot Mountain

Pilot Mountain stands watch,
a lonely sentinel guarding
the Sauratown Mountains to the east
and the Blue Ridge to the north.
In the easy hills of the Piedmont,
the heavens bend down to touch
the stoney knob.

As I pass, the mountain says:
Follow me and I will show you
the edge of the world;
listen and I will show you
hawk and deer,
          wind and moon;
look and I will show you
the way home.

And now if you quiet your heart,
I will give you my odd blessing.
I will show you
the darkness of your Self.

Then, and only then
will you know:

          You are forgiven.
          You have always been forgiven.

Everything You Need

Have you ever seen the rainbow
explode into the sky?

Have you ever driven
through one so her colors drip
over you and you are
covered in blue and green and indigo?

Have you ever touched orange and yellow
so full of power that you thought
you were living in a dream?

Have you ever seen the clouds
part like a curtain and the moon
in her fullness come out to bow?

Have you ever felt the moon
shine her light into your cells
and you shiver in every
crevice of your soul?

Have you ever heard the moon laugh?

Have you ever stopped and
looked up into the heavens,
not to see a tornado, but a promise?

Have you ever heard the rainbow whisper,
You have everything you need?

Turning from Troy

In middle age all men are Odysseus,
wanting to go home
after fighting at Troy
for more years than can be counted.

Our Troys are not walled cities
but office and cubicle, shop and
job site, factory and field.
These battlefields are strewn with
the broken, wounded, and slain.

In our beserker rage, we fight but
do not know what for . . .
          maybe a paycheck, maybe a promotion.
Glory is far away, not to be had.
Honor is fleeting
and our dear friends like Ajax are lost.

Patroclus is dead.

And so are Hal, Charlie, Tony,
Stephen, and Craig.

At some point we know the war is over.
We turn from Troy.

The journey home is long and treacherous.
Many perish along the way.
Our bodies are tired and ache.
Pain in our souls is a constant companion
for we know our youth is over,

gone for ever.

We are seduced by shiny things.
Many are devoured by monsters;
others drown in whirlpools.
We escape Cyclops

only to find the Laistrygonians waiting.

We are tempted by Sirens
and captured by desires.
We are smashed on the rocks

of divorce and addiction, depression
and heart attack, apathy and lethargy.

Thunderbolts from Zeus and
storms from Poseidon
wreck our lives.

But still we turn toward home,
our Ithaca.
There, always there,
if the gods have smiled on us
is our beloved companion of all the years,
the one who has loved us
when we felt ruined,

who healed us with a forgiving embrace,
who showed us the way of laughter.

We turn toward the beloved,
toward home
also knowing that we turn,
mercifully,
towards death

                    now ours.

Winter

The earth needs to tilt away
from the sun every now and then
so the days are short, the nights
long and deep, and winter cold drives
through the land. The far-away stars
watch carefully.

Like us all, the earth needs the rest
given by the cold night and the return of quiet.
Like the earth, we all have the need to tilt away
and turn towards something else.

I try to stop the manic doing of trying
to prove my worth. I wish I could lay
down a burden or two and find sweet
release. I want to know that in the winter
of my tilting away, my heart will not freeze
like a pipe under the sink.

Credo

I believe in
second chances,
and poetry,
and tears,

       and angels too.

I believe in
home,
and stories,
and dreams,

       and mercy most of all,

sweet,

       life-giving

mercy.

God Is Dead . . . Again

It's happened again.
God has died.

The Church is now
an anxiety-laden husk, an
empty shell, kept alive
on life-support at all
costs by the hand-wringing
princes in power.

The language is bankrupt,
having lost its meaning
along the way. The great
paradigm of life-death-
resurrection doesn't hold
anymore for the Institution.

There are too many jobs
at stake, too much property to
care about, and too many
pensions needing funding.

God died slowly this time,
real slow.

Oh well.

Prepare ye the way of the Lord.

Homemade Cookies

The door slams open,
the noise and laughter follow—
hungry teenagers growing
into their bodies and their selves.

Like heat-seeking missiles, they hone in
on the cookie jar. They swarm and
a wild feeding frenzy ensues. The cookies
waiting for them are warm, right out

of the oven . . . maybe chocolate chip or oatmeal,
or the famous snicker-doodles, maybe chapel cookies.
Warm cookies and a glass of cold milk
comprise heaven on earth.

The secret recipe for homemade cookies
calls for kindness, a touch of tenderness,
a smattering of respect, and an abundance
of care and forgiveness—and laughter.

Don't forget the laughter.
In the coming hardness of
their growing up,
I hope these teenagers
                remember.

Hawk

for Terri Kuczynski

I watch you
walk your dog in the mornings.
You are wary of me,
curious and wondering:
Will I attack and eat you?
Or will I just
fly away and leave?

I see your
Sorrow and Pain.
I know you have carried
these two friends of mine a long way.
And so it shall be.

I have come to tell you:

You are my beloved daughter.
All shall be well.

Phoenix

I believe there are three things
needed in order to begin recovering
from the trauma of being
in a house fire.

1.
There is Grief. Grief is not only necessary;
it is required. After the shock and numbness
wear off—and it is acceptable to be in shock
and to be numb—comes a bucket full of grief with
all the tears, slobber, and snot, fear and terror.
There is no escape. Anger wells up from
surprising places, looking for a place to land and
a fight to pick. Fatigue and stress rule and sleep
is hard. Then comes the sharp pains of
remembering what was lost, and the hot
resentment of all the details required now.
There are no short cuts, no quick fixes.
There is no easy way out.

2.
So Patience is needed, needed now more than
ever. Recovering takes time and a
certain difficult waiting and a willingness
to slow down and be depleted, and live into
the hard work of remembering and feeling.
Dreams ask for care and gentleness as they
come in all their weirdness bringing the hope
of healing. Dreams are angels. Be kind to them.
As best you can, endure the love and care from
others that sweeps over you. Let your dear
friends help carry the heavy load.

3.

A full measure of Laughter is required.
Do not be afraid of laughter. Let yourself be
sheltered in a lightness of step and of heart.
You no longer have to account for all the accumulated
unnecessary stuff; you no longer have to feel
guilty about possessions. Let the absurdity capture
a new realization of gratitude. Have a chuckle
about how good it feels to travel lighter and
easier. Smile as you cuddle your spouse at
night, marveling at what you now know about
what matters most, about how your
life is changing and is changed, how
your life is marked forever,

not only by fire but
by a shadowy phoenix.

Night Thunder

During the hour of the wolf,
the far-away drums beat
loud enough to wake you.
You feel the storm coming
with its low roar and shaking
of trees. A shot of adrenaline
surges through. Your body
remembers the thunder, the
bombardment of rain, the lightning
strike, the hissing fire.
You look at the ceiling,
stomach churning, mouth dry
with the taste of fear, mind racing:
make sure your family and the dog are safe,
glasses are on the bedside table,
wallet on the dresser.

Fight the monster as best you can and
be sure to close doors on the way out.

I am shaking as the night thunders.

Prelude to the Great War

I. Shiloh
In April of 1862 Shiloh was no longer a place of peace,
but a place where the Beast was set loose
upon the new nation, conceived in liberty
and dedicated to the proposition that all
men were created equal—
or so the President said later.
The silent monuments resting on the battlefield
cannot speak to the devouring that took place
at the Sunken Road and Hornet's Nest
and in the Peach Orchard.
The Beast spat out the dead and wounded
in the forests and fields,
around the Bloody Pond.

It was not enough; it is never enough.
The Beast will never be filled.

There was no victory or defeat at Shiloh,
only a snarling madness
that hollows out a man
forever.

II. Franklin
> *If we are to die,*
>
> *let us die like men.*
>
> —*Major General Patrick Cleburne*

As the battle ended, four dead Confederate generals
were laid out on the back porch
of the Carnton Plantation-turned-hospital.
Dead generals are special.

They get books written about their lives,
their leadership, and their errors.
Dead Confederate generals have their
busts on pedestals at the Visitors Center.

But the grunts just spread out into a line of battle
and begin the long slow march toward
the Union fortifications. There they will be cut down
and slaughtered. Simple as that.

The bullets and miniballs will rip into flesh,
cannon will turn some boys into a fine red mist.
These soldiers will not lie in honor on the porch
with a small white cloth over their face.

They end up in graves marked
Unknown Confederate Soldier.
There will be no books written of their courage,
no busts on pedestals,

just grave after grave at the Carnton Plantation
tended with care by Mrs. McGavock
while the mothers in the far-off countries
like Mississippi and Arkansas keen.

And the fathers, well . . .
they swallow
their grief and choke.

For the Pain

It might be shots of whiskey,
six packs of beer, or
bottles of wine—
 anything not to feel.

It might be bad junk food,
numbing video games, or
soul-stealing pornography—
 anything not to feel.

It might be hours of unimportant work,
different kinds of pills, or
miles of exhausting exercise—
 anything not to feel.

It might be placing bets,
getting addicted to Jesus, or
shopping for things not needed—
 anything not to feel.

You know all the strategies to distract,
to deaden the pain,
to keep the anxiety away.
It's easier to endure the shame
than feel the pain.
But the gods demand something
different from you now.
They do not want your shame.
They demand a sacrifice of your numbness
for the sake of your soul.
They say: Find a poem that turns
you upside down and brings tears.
Read it out loud.
Read it out loud over and over again.

Read it out loud to people who love you.
Give your pain to the poem—

    anything to feel.

Sweet Release

April 1, 2014

Death came at last
and spoke softly to my mother:

It is time to come with me.
God is waiting for you.
You have done enough here.
You have said goodbye.
You have loved your family.
It is time to let go.
They will be brave.
They will miss you

but you no longer need to stay here.
The party is about to begin.

Hook Shot

Dad arrives from his office, late afternoon.
He's been seeing patients all day.
The walking sick and the worried well, he calls them.
He parks his Corvair up the driveway,
leaving room around the basketball goal.

My brother and I are going at it one-on-one.
It's our usual brutal game with lots of pushing,
shoving, hacking, bumping.
We play a full-body contact sport here.
It's a no-blood, no-foul kind of game.

I throw a hard bounce pass to Dad.
He sets his medicine bag down
and we double team him,
up so close I can smell his office and
feel his strength and wisdom.

He takes a flat-footed hook shot
as we try to block it.
The ball arches high, kisses off the backboard
nothing but net.
He laughs and heads in the backdoor.

I am left wanting.
I wish I had been able to bang up
against him more as I was growing up.
If I had, I wonder if I would
miss him as much as I do now.

The Music of Heaven

Bach plays in heaven,
and Mannheim Steamroller
during winter solstice,
and, of course, the Beatles.

But when the angels need
to smile,
they listen for Kelli's
laughter.

Her laughter comes from
a wellspring of gladness,
from a deep place
of delight,
of joy,
of ease,
of wonder.

Born out of loss
and the knowing of
God's acceptance,
Kelli's laughter
is the music
of heaven.